PASSIONS...

Sailing

PASSIONS...

Sailing

PHOTOGRAPHS SUPPLIED BY KOS PICTURE SOURCE

DREAM PLACES YOU'D RATHER BE

DUNCAN BAIRD PUBLISHERS

LONDON

PASSIONS... Sailing

First published in the United Kingdom and
Ireland in 2006 by
Duncan Baird Publishers Ltd
Sixth Floor
Castle House
75–76 Wells Street
London W1T 3QH

Conceived, created and designed by
Duncan Baird Publishers

Managing Editor: Yvonne Worth
Managing Designer: Suzanne Tuhrim
Picture Researcher: Louise Glasson
Foreword: Brian Steel

British Library Cataloguing-in-Publication Data:
A CIP record for this book is available from
the British Library

ISBN-10: 1-84483-336-4
ISBN-13: 9-781844-833368

10 9 8 7 6 5 4 3 2 1

Typeset in Bergell and Futura
Colour reproduction by Colourscan, Singapore
Printed in Singapore by Imago

Foreword

IF EVER INSPIRATION WERE NEEDED TO ANSWER
THE CALL OF THE SEA, IT CAN BE FOUND IN THESE
WORDS BY MARK TWAIN.

*"Twenty years from now you will be more disappointed by the
things you didn't do than by the ones you did do. So throw
off the bowlines. Sail away from the safe harbor. Catch
the trade winds in your sails. Explore. Dream. Discover."*

TWAIN'S WORDS MAY WELL HAVE BEEN INTENDED
TO CONVEY A BROADER PHILOSOPHY OF LIFE IN

GENERAL, BUT TO ANYONE WITH A TASTE FOR THE SEA THEY CAN MEAN ONLY ONE THING – SAILING.

WHAT BETTER ANALOGY COULD THERE BE TO ENCOURAGE US TO THROW OFF OUR RESTRAINTS, ESCAPE THE PRESSURES OF EVERYDAY LIFE AND FOLLOW OUR DREAMS.

DREAMS OF A WORLD THAT IS AT ONE WITH NATURE, DREAMS THAT EVOKE THE JOY OF HARNESSING THE WIND AND THE EXCITEMENT OF MAKING LANDFALL, WHETHER IT IS ACROSS THE BAY OR ON THE OTHER SIDE OF THE GLOBE.

WEEKENDERS AND WORLDWIDE WANDERERS, BUOY RACERS AND HARBOUR HOPPERS ALIKE, WE SAILORS ALL SHARE A COMMON BOND – A DEEP LOVE OF BEING ON THE WATER.

OUR HEARTS ARE UPLIFTED BY THE EXHILARATION OF RAISING SAIL AND THE RITUALS OF HONOURING THE MOOD-SWINGS OF WIND, WAVES AND WEATHER. WE SAIL, AND TAKE OUR FORTUNE AS IT COMES. WE ABSORB OURSELVES IN THE MOMENT. UNTIL AT LAST, ONCE THE ADVENTURE IS OVER, WE SETTLE SAFELY AT ANCHOR, MOORING OR BERTH AND RELIVE OUR ADVENTURES OVER A CHEERING GLASS.

THE THRILL OF A FIRST ATLANTIC CROSSING, THE DELIGHT OF SAILING PAST THE STATUE OF LIBERTY INTO NEW YORK, THE AWESOME RAGE OF A HURRICANE ARE ALL CHERISHED EXPERIENCES OF A SPIRITUAL DIMENSION. YET, JUST AS PROFOUND, AND EQUALLY ENRICHING FOR THE SOUL, ARE THE HOURS SPENT FLOATING GENTLY IN HOME WATERS.

THE MOST CASUAL DAY OUT AND THE MOST COMPLEX LONG-HAUL VOYAGES ALL BEGIN IN THE SAME WAY ... READY THAT BOWLINE?

"The true peace of God begins at any point 1,000 miles from the nearest land."

JOSEPH CONRAD (1857–1924)

"There never was a great man yet who spent all his life inland."

HERMAN MELVILLE (1819-91)

"Ships are the nearest things
to dreams that hands
have ever made,
For somewhere deep in their
oaken hearts the soul
of a song is laid."

ROBERT N. ROSE

21

"Don't set sail on someone else's star."

AFRICAN PROVERB

24

"Wisdom sails with wind and time."

JOHN FLORIO (1553–1625)

"He that will not sail till all dangers are over must never put to sea."

THOMAS FULLER (1608–61)

"Thought is the wind,
knowledge the sail, and
mankind the vessel."

AUGUST HARE (1792–1834)

"It was with a happy heart that the good Odysseus spread his sail to catch the wind and used his seamanship to keep his boat straight ..."

HOMER (C. 700 BC)

"... steer for the deep
waters only. ...
For we are bound
where mariner has not
yet dared go."

WALT WHITMAN (1819–92)

"Man cannot discover new oceans unless he has the courage to lose sight of the shore."

ANDRÉ GIDE (1869–1951)

"'Tis the set of the sail that decides the goal, and not the storm of life."

ELLA WHEELER WILCOX (1850–1919)

"We cannot command Nature except by obeying her."

FRANCIS BACON (1561–1626)

"You never enjoy the world aright, till the sea itself floweth in your veins, till you are clothed with the heavens and crowned with the stars."

THOMAS TRAHERNE (1636–74)

"The world is an ocean,
our hearts are its shores."

CHINESE PROVERB

"I'm not afraid of storms,
for I'm learning how to
sail my ship."

LOUISA MAY ALCOTT (1832–88)

"The real voyage of
discovery consists not
of seeking new landscapes,
but in having new eyes ..."

MARCEL PROUST (1871–1922)

"A smooth sea never made
a skilled mariner."

ENGLISH PROVERB

"The pessimist complains about the wind; the optimist expects it to change; the realist adjusts the sails."

WILLIAM ARTHUR WARD (1921–94)

"A ship in harbour is safe,
but that is not what ships
are built for."

WILLIAM SHEDD (1820–94)

"Let the beauty we love
be what we do."

RUMI (1207–73)

Locations

Text credits

page 21 Robert N. Rose, from the poem "Ships".
Inscription held in State Library of Victoria, Australia.
page 58 André Gide, from *The Counterfeiters* (1925).
English translation copyright © Alfred A. Knopf Inc., 1927.
page 83 Marcel Proust, widely quoted.
page 92 William Arthur Ward, from the poem "To Risk".

Picture credits

All photographs from Kos Picture Source www.kospictures.com
All photographs taken by Kos except for the following

PHOTOGRAPHERS:
page 5 Alexis Andrews; **12** Gilles Martin-Raget; **14–15** Carlo
Borlenghi; **18–19** Carlo Borlenghi; **22–23** Gilles Martin-Raget;
26–27 Tom Bol; **28–29** Peter McGowan; **30–31** Carlo Borlenghi;
33 Jens Fischer; **34** Carlo Borlenghi; **36–37** Gilles Martin-Raget;
48–49 Gary John Norman; **54–55** Carlo Borlenghi; **59** Gilles
Martin-Raget; **70–71** Gary John Norman; **78** Alexis Andrews;
81 Jessica Dobbs; **82** Carlo Borlenghi; **84–85** Gary John Norman;
86–87 Carlo Borlenghi; **89** Gilles Martin-Raget; **94–95** Carlo
Borlenghi; **100–101** Gilles Martin-Raget; **104–105** Jessica Dobbs;
107 Guido Cantini.